KABBALAH

Find more books by Rabbi Yaakov HaLevi in the Jewish Wisdom Series by V'Hai Bahem - Elixir of Life Publications including

The Messiah
Strangers? (on Jewish Conversion)
Judaism and the Occult
The Law of the Land
Torah: For the Nations?

KABBALAH

How It Transformed the Jewish World and
Continues To Ignite the Search for God

◆◆◆

V'Hai Bahem - Elixir of Life Publications

◆◆◆

Part of the
JEWISH WISDOM SERIES

Rabbi Yaakov HaLevi S"T

Printed in the United States of America
First Printing, 2021

V'Hai Bahem - Elixir of Life Publications
vhaibahem@gmail.com

Dedicated to my wife, children, grandchildren, the sponsors of this project, and all those who seek the Truth of the Creator's Torah.

Contents

1 - Introduction & Early History

Many people ask me what Kabbalah is. Is it a part of Torah? If it is, why don't most people study it, including most rabbis? Why do some oppose it? Is it taken into consideration when deciding Jewish Law (halachah)? Is it one book, or many? Are there different kinds of Kabbalah? Is it consistent with the Talmud?

First, we must understand that the Torah is seen has having layers of meaning. Much like an onion, when a level is peeled away, we find another layer, then another. There are infinite layers in the Torah. There is a verse in *Psalms* that says, "The Torah of God is *temimah*." Temimah is usually translated as "perfect," but another meaning is "untouched." Despite thousands of years of study and analysis, we have barely scratched its depths. We generally divide these layers into four groups; *peshat*: the simple, literal meaning; *drash*: homiletics (interpreting the spiritual, moral implications of the words); *remez*: allegory; and *sod*: secret, mystical meanings. The acronym of these is *PaRDeS*, which means "an orchard." An analogy sometimes given is that of a pound of coal. One can burn it and heat a room for an hour. One can unlock the atomic bonds in the coal and heat a city for a month. There are different approaches to Kabbalah, in different eras, in different groups, with different goals.

Reading the Bible or Talmud casually would lead one to conclude that there had been no such thing as Kabbalah in those days. But let's look more carefully. The first chapter of *Ezekiel* deals with a vision the prophet had of a throne, shapes of animals, mysterious winds, fire wheels… without a word of explanation. In the Talmud, we read,

"One should not study the *Work of Creation* with three, nor the *Work of the Chariot* even with one, unless he is wise and understands by himself."

What? Creation is outlined in the beginning of Genesis. The Chariot? (Ezekiel's vision) is also in scripture. Who does not know these things? The Talmud understands these two topics as being a sort of code — the mysteries of creation and the mysteries of what is above creation; the higher realities — but the Talmud has an ominous story. Four of the greatest rabbis entered the "Orchard." One lost his life, one lost his mind, one lost his faith, and only one (Rabbi Akiva) entered and departed in peace. Not everyone may enter the hidden chambers. This section of the Talmud is actually only a snippet of a vast literature known as the *Heichalot* (palaces). Many rabbis of the Talmud who appear as legalists and ethicists were actually involved in mystical investigations of the meaning of the world and that which is beyond.

They would meditate, go into trances, and see visions of the higher worlds, especially Ezekiel's Chariot, which was seen as the blueprint of the universe. They would report to their students gathered around them about what they were seeing and hearing. Some of our standard prayers are actually from the Heichalot literature. The song *E-l Adon*, sung in virtually every synagogue on Shabbat morning, originates from this literature. But it was seen as dangerous. Not even every rabbi of the Talmud dared approach the Throne of God. The Heichalot literature was known but kept from the masses.

Numerous other works were kept even more hidden. Rabbi Judah the Pious (c. 1200) writes of people keeping ancient manuscripts in special arks, with olive oil lamps kept burning before them. It would not contribute to the honor of God if these mysteries became common fare. This was soon to change, however.

◆◆◆

2 - Schools of the Middle Ages

In the Middle Ages, several forms of Kabbalah developed, all rooted in the original Kabbalah of our sages. In France and Germany, the Kabbalists emphasized humility, awe for the Names of God, connecting various mitzvot (commandments) with Divine Names, and meditating on these names while performing these mitzvot. However, it was still the province of the learned.

Spain was particularly fertile ground for Kabbalah. Although some shunned Kabbalah in favor of "rationalistic" philosophy, Kabbalah was the main spiritual outlook of Spanish Jews at the time. There were many who also tried to reconcile Kabbalah with philosophy, and who came up with a lot of deep, original thought. Of the Kabbalists, there were two main approaches in Spain. One, similar to the German Kabbalah, emphasized Divine Names. But they went much further; they would meditate on the letters until they experienced an illumination. Some even called it a prophecy. One famous rabbi of this school even developed a "Jewish yoga," replete with breathing exercises and special postures, all connected with Divine Names.

Another school of Spanish Kabbalah delved into theosophy (the philosophy of knowing God). The traditions of the Chariot Mystics (Yordei Hamerkavah) were elaborated upon. God Himself is unknowable and transcendent. He has no name and is simply called *Ein Sof* (Infinite). It is Ein Sof, and Ein Sof alone, that we mean when we say God. Ein Sof emitted a ray of His light, and, like a ray of sunlight hitting a prism, there became differentiated "attributes," alluded to in *1 Chronicles 29:10-13*. These are known as the Ten Sefirot (which may mean "Spheres" or "Lights"). It is through the Sefirot that we may have a perception of God, but they are no more God than a ray of sunlight is the Sun.

All the names by which God is known relate to our perceptions of Him in the Sephirot. Our world exists at the "bottom" of the Sefirot. (This is all a tremendous simplification). Just as there are the Holy Sefirot, there are also the unholy. There was meant to be a balance, but when man sins, there is a hemorrhaging of the light of God into the Sefirot of Evil. This is called "The exile of the divine presence (Galut HaShechinah). Sin causes a "disconnect" between different "levels" within God, God and the world, God and man, and man within himself. This is the root cause of human suffering. These ideas were not just among the scholars but became part of the understanding of Judaism for Spanish Jews.

Then, in 1492, after at least nine hundred years of Spanish-Jewish life, mostly with peace and freedom, the Spanish Jews were exiled, hounded by the Inquisition. Many went to Portugal, but the same thing happened there four years later. The Spanish Jews went from riches to rags. They had been a prosperous, spiritually enlightened community for so long, but were now left to wander, penniless. The question was, "*Why?*" The philosophers had no answers. Most of them became humanists. But the Kabbalists had an answer: it was the exile of the divine presence. We are reliving the cosmic drama on a human level. We need to perform Tikkun-repair on ourselves, repair on the universe. But how? A recently discovered book would tell them, and they would apply it in a new home.

◆◆◆

3 - *The Zohar* is Revealed

We left off with the exile of Spanish Jewry. They were scattered to many lands; some to Europe (particularly Amsterdam) but mostly to Mediterranean countries. The Turkish Empire especially welcomed them. The sultan of Turkey said, "The king of Spain has impoverished his land and enriched mine."

Many settled in the Holy Land, particularly in the city of Safed (Tzfat), which by the early 1500s boasted some fifteen thousand Jews, mostly Spanish refugees. Among them were Talmudic scholars, codifiers, and Kabbalists. I mentioned at the end of the previous post that they were in possession of a wonderful book. This was the *Zohar*, the Book of Splendor. It had appeared in Spain just before 1300. It is a Kabalistic Midrash, a running narrative on the Torah, based on Kabbalistic ideas. It was attributed to Rabbi Shimon Bar Yochai, a great second century rabbi. Whether this attribution is accurate, or whether it had only been composed in the late thirteenth century, or was an ancient work that had gone through substantial editing over the ages, has been a subject of controversy ever since. Even Rabbi Nachman, who revered the book, said it was impossible to ascribe the entire work to Rabbi Shimon Bar Yochai, especially as it quoted the words of many much later rabbis.

Be that as it may, it is a most remarkable work with incredible depth, which was cherished by the last two centuries of Spanish Kabbalists. It speaks of future events, hidden meanings of the mitzvot, and especially of effecting a Tikkun; a repair or rectification of the universe. The new exiles, especially those who had chosen to live in the Land of Israel, dove into the depths of this book in order to understand the meaning of their woes and how to reverse them.

The greatest of these was Rabbi Isaac Luria, known as the Ari (1534-1572). His father, a German Jew, died when he was an infant. His mother, an Egyptian Jew, took her son with her to live with her family in Egypt. When he married, his father-in-law arranged for him a place to live on the banks of the Nile, so he could immerse often, and hired nine Jews to stay with him, so he would always have a prayer quorum (minyan). He delved deeper and deeper into the *Zohar*, and had the Prophet Elijah revealed to him. Once, Elijah told him: "Know, that your time in this world is almost up. You have come into this world to teach one person, Rabbi Hayyim Vital, and he will teach the entire world. You must go to Safed to find him." He moved to Safed, where he lived another year and a half, passing away at the age of thirty-eight. Rabbi Hayyim was his constant companion.

The Ari heard messages from God, not only through the holy books, but in the sound of the wind, the chirping of birds everywhere. He would look at a person and tell them what they had done wrong and how to correct it. He would reveal past lives to people and inform them why they had come back; what was left undone. He would comment on customs; sometimes preferring an Ashkenazic custom, sometimes a Sephardic, sometimes saying a particular thing could be done either way, sometimes saying that both were wrong and something entirely different should be done. His writing consisted of only a few hymns, but Rabbi Hayyim Vital wrote what he had heard. The edition that I have fills an entire shelf. People flocked from all over, even Muslim clergy, to hear his wisdom. He hinted that he was the reincarnation of Moses and Rabbi Shimon Bar Yochai. Besides the ordinary practices, he introduced several new ones, aimed at

"Raising up the Divine Presence from the dust." He elaborated on the *Zohar's* teaching about the Sefirot.

There were not just ten, but numerous sub-sefirot and combinations of Sefirot, which made God appear to have different "faces" at different times. He also posited an "empty space" between God and the first Sefirot, which gives God the appearance of transcendence; although, in reality, he is very imminent, always. He saw all things in terms of "sparks" of God, which needed to be raised, effecting that object's Tikkun and contributing to the Tikkun of the universe. The Ari's teachings spread far and wide in the Jewish world (although the authentic version of Rabbi Hayyim Vital arrived in Europe only in the mid-eighteenth century). Middle Eastern Jews, especially, accepted him completely, and adjusted their practices accordingly, but every Jewish community adopted the Ari's teachings and instructions to one degree or another. Redemption seemed nearer than ever. But then, tragedy struck.

◆◆◆

4 - The Disaster of Shabbetai Tzvi

We left off at the spread of Kabbalah that followed the renown of the Ari. In every corner of the Jewish world, Kabbalah had gone mainstream, and spiritual renewal was in the air. Even in Christian circles, Kabbalah was "reinterpreted" in terms of their own theology (Sir Isaac Newton was a major proponent of this movement), but the seventeenth century brought many disasters.

In 1648 and 1649, the Jews of Ukraine were caught in the middle of an uprising of Ukrainians against their Polish overlords. An estimated hundred thousand Jews were murdered (some put the figure at five hundred thousand). Many were tortured as well. Atrocities of every kind were perpetrated. The leader of the uprising, Bogdan Chmielnitzki, is still considered a hero in Ukraine. His statue can be seen everywhere, and his likeness is on the five-hryvnia note.

Jews who hadn't lost their lives, lost their property. Learning halted for a long time among Ukrainian Jews. Nothing like this had happened since the Crusades, some four hundred years earlier, and nothing like it would happen again until the Holocaust, some three hundred years later.

When Jews go through things like this, Messiah fever takes hold. Several individuals arose claiming to be the Messiah but were laughed off. All except one.

Shabbetai Tzvi was born in Smyrna, Turkey in 1626. By all accounts, he was a charismatic person with a remarkable singing voice. (I can't help making comparisons with Shlomo Carlebach. They even looked very much alike). He became an accomplished scholar. He apparently suffered from what today we would call bipolar syndrome. In his "down phase," he was a pious Jew. In his "up phase," he committed sins, primarily the pronouncing of the ultimate Divine Name, which is considered a grave sin, and the eating of forbidden animal fats. When he was out of the "up phase," he deeply regretted his actions and was plagued by guilt. He was deeply troubled by the events of 1648 and 1649 and began to feel that he was the long-awaited Messiah. He was banished by the rabbis of Smyrna and began wanderings through the Middle East and the Balkans. He continued to do bizarre things. He had several marriages, but none were consummated. He married a Torah scroll as well.

Although he was not taken seriously by most, he did attract a following. Finally, he met Nathan of Gaza (yes, Jews did live in Gaza), a well-respected Kabbalist. Shabbetai sought help for his mental illness. Nathan told him that, in fact, he was the Messiah. Nathan formulated a theory that the soul of the Messiah dwelled in the "empty space" spoken of by the Ari. It had gone through unspeakable tortures since creation, which accounted for his mental pain. This included terrifying dragons and the soul of Jesus.

Nathan also theorized that the fallen sparks, which the Ari had spoken of, had already been elevated, and there only remained sparks which had fallen all the way into evil. The Messiah would need to sin in order to reach these. However, these sins were only for the Messiah. Others had to continue observing halachah, except in a few areas. Nathan sent pamphlets throughout the world, even reaching the few Jews in the Americas.

1666 would be the year of redemption. Two years of mass hysteria ensued. People everywhere began "prophesying." Even many rabbis were taken in, as well as many, if not most, Jews (this is greatly downplayed in most popular books). Rabbinic figures revered even today announced that people should not be dismayed by Shabbetai's sins, as "He knows the root of the matter" (i.e., the inner, mystical meanings of his actions).

Great fights occurred in Jewish communities like Amsterdam and Constantinople. The few rabbis who opposed him were the constant objects of death threats. Christian Europe was in a panic, as rumor had it that Shabbetai had raised a great army, which had already destroyed Mecca and was now marching on Rome. Shabbetai went back to Turkey, with the express idea of converting the Sultan to Judaism. The Sultan had him put in prison. No problem, wrote Nathan. This is part of his descent into the dark realm.

1666 would change everything. When 1666 arrived, the Sultan gave Shabbetai the option of death or conversion to Islam. He chose conversion. Jews were stunned. The expected deliverance would not occur! Most of his followers abandoned him. Jewish communities everywhere readily accepted back those who had followed him, as it had been an honest, and widespread, mistake.

But it didn't end there. Nathan wrote that Shabbetai's apostasy was part of his mission, a further decent into evil, in order to destroy it from within. *Just wait. It will be okay.* But it wasn't. Shabbetai was given a prison island where he lived and received visitors. While outwardly a Muslim, he secretly maintained a semi-Jewish lifestyle. Of those who visited him, he commanded many to convert to Islam as well, but with the intent of restoring the sparks. These followers became part of a new religion, the Donmeh, which still exists in Turkey.

In 2000, I joined a lovely tour in Istanbul by the local Jewish community. The guide was a nice, soft-spoken man, but when I asked him if there is any interaction between the Jewish Community and the Donmeh, he screamed an emphatic, "No!"

As Shabbetai begun signing his name as "the God of Israel," many Donmeh considered him to be God, but within the Jewish community, many of his followers stayed Jews, awaiting his return in glory from "the realm of evil" at any moment. At his death just a few years later, most abandoned hope. But not all. Some expected his return. Some Jews, even rabbis, behaved outwardly as devout Jews but secretly believed the Messiah had come and the laws of the Torah were now abrogated.

A generation later, a Polish Jew, Jacob Frank, proclaimed himself the reincarnation of Shabbetai Tzvi. Together with some ten thousand followers, he convinced the Bishop of Cracow to baptize them, as they believed the Messiah had come. The Bishop assumed he meant Jesus, but he actually meant himself. As opposed to Shabbetai, he encouraged his followers to sin in any way possible in order to reach the sparks that had fallen low. But the sins were not just eating forbidden fats. Incest and adultery were high on his agenda. They believed that once everything was destroyed, a new and better world would appear.

Frankist cells continued to exist from the early eighteenth century to as late as World War I. Some believe they still exist, but I have not seen any evidenced for this. Frankists heavily influenced some modern Jewish movements, particularly Reform, and, to a lesser extent, Zionism. The great historian of Kabbalah, Gershom Scholem, even saw a Frankist background to Hasidism, but this view has now been largely abandoned by scholars.

Besides the trauma of dashed hopes, the Jewish people now had to worry if their friends and neighbors might be secret Sabbeteans or Frankists. Often, like witch hunts, innocent people were brought under suspicion along with the guilty. As both the followers of Shabbetai and Frank had based themselves on a perversion of Kabbalistic ideas, many became wary of Kabbalah in general. How this was handled in different Jewish communities, and the effects that are still felt, will be the topic of my next post.

◆◆◆

5 - Kabbalah's Reception Changes

The Sabbatean and Frankist debacles had torn us apart and made us paranoid about our neighbors and even our rabbis. The responses varied, and a new climate was created, not always for the better. Many of our present problems stem from those long-ago traumas.

In Western Europe, every effort was made to jettison the Kabbalah. Where Kabbalistic customs were already well established, they were kept but de-emphasized. This is why in most Ashkenazi communities, when reciting the Kabbalat Shabbat prayers, the reader steps away from his usual podium for the very Kabbalistic *Lecha Dodi*, showing that it isn't "really" a part of the prayers. In Amsterdam, the most open of European cities at the time and a major battle ground between Sabbateans and anti-Sabbateans, Kabbalah was simply banned. I had heard that there was an official *herem* (a ban on excommunication) in Amsterdam for anyone studying or practicing Kabbalistic rites. I wrote an email several years ago to the head of the Amsterdam Jewish community asking about this. He said, "I don't know if there is a formal *herem*, but we do absolutely nothing in accordance with the Kabbalah." Interestingly, the community records for Amsterdam have the years 1665 and 1666 simply torn out of the ledger. But it doesn't end with this.

Moses Mendelssohn of Germany founded the so-called "Enlightenment," which sought a Jewish spirituality while abandoning those rituals that set us apart from others and resulted in the creation of Reform Judaism. Every one of his close followers was a Frankist. A non-observant Judaism resonated with them (this has been well documented by twentieth century historians).

So, a secular, or at least a non-observant, interpretation of Judaism, if not originating in Sabbateanism, was successful due to it (Note: This in no way implies that non-Orthodox Jews today are knowingly Sabbatean).

In Eastern Europe, Enlightenment gave birth to a secular, cultural interpretation of Judaism. When Herzl formulated his theory of Zionism, especially with its interpretation by Max Nordau (that religion is now a bad thing), it struck a responsive chord in many East European Jews. Socialism and communism, both "Messianic," antinomian (against Law) visions, were readily adopted by Russian Jews. Lenin's inner circle was almost all Jews. Eastern European immigrants to America were mostly socialists. In this way, Shabbetai and Jacob Frank live on in left wing "progressive" American politics.

Middle Eastern Jews took the attitude, "Okay, we made a big mistake. Let's go back to where we were." Kabbalah remains central in these communities. If one visits a Middle Eastern style Sepharadic synagogue, there will likely be a class on *Zohar* between the afternoon and evening service. Even Sabbatean rituals and prayers that had "gotten in" were tolerated, as long as they were not blatantly heretical. A good example is the Tu B'Shvat "seder." The Sabbateans had made a special ritual of reciting various Talmudic and kabbalistic passages, along with consuming fruit on this day, which is the "New Year of the Trees." First, fruit was eaten that was totally edible, then fruit with an inedible pit, then fruit with an inedible outer shell. The forces of evil are referred to in Kabbalah as "shells" (*klipot*). This ritual was meant to indicate a journey starting with good, then hidden evil, and concluding with blatant evil, which could and should be entered. Most

Middle East Sepharadim follow this ritual even today, but without reference to Sabbatean concepts. It's just a fruit celebration. No need was felt to eliminate it (I oppose it).

In Central and Eastern Europe, a more moderate approach was taken. Kabbalah is great, but let's put it back to where it is only for scholars. It is too dangerous for the average person. Communities allotted space for Kabbalists to gather, pray, and study. But now, one had to be at least forty years old, married, and with a solid knowledge of Talmud. This would insure stability. The Kabbalistic writings of the rabbis in this tradition do not deal with emotions, revelations, redemption, etc., but rather with deep interpretations of the Bible and Talmud, inspired by Kabbalah. Ethical literature of this period is also replete with Kabbalah. But the experiential was gone.

Great yeshivot were founded that dealt with everyday, practical, as well as theoretical Judaism, but the transcendental was usually lacking. The rabbis now feared a religion based too much on emotion. The masses were not pleased. They longed for spiritual awakening. Most did not feel their needs were being addressed. The time was right for a revolution of sorts. It did come, in the form of Hasidism.

◆◆◆

6 - Hasidism is Born

Rabbi Israel Baal Shem Tov (the Master of the Good Name) (1698–1760) appeared on the stage of history at this time. There are so many legends, that it is difficult to distinguish fact from fiction. At least one early twentieth century historian even concluded that he was a totally legendary figure. However, since the fall of the Iron Curtain, scholars have had access to old Polish and Ukrainian records, which have cast a great deal of light on the man, his ideas, and his actions.

He lived in Medzhibuzh, which is now in Ukraine but at one time was in Poland, close to the border of the Russian Empire. I have visited there many times. There is an old fortress, now a museum, that commemorates Jewish, Polish, and Ukrainian cultures in that town.

There is a long-standing controversy over whether or not Rabbi Israel was a scholar. Many documents have surfaced in the last few years showing that indeed he was, although not in the Lithuanian sense of being overanalytical. Books of legal material frequently quoted him, and rabbis made their rulings contingent on his approval. No contemporary document has been found that is critical of him. The legends of local or far-reaching opposition have been proven false, with evidence that he was loved by both Jew and gentile. He was, in fact, an heir to the medieval German "Hasidim." They were pious and could affect miracles by using Divine Names in amulets, or simply by meditating on these Names.

He differed, however, in that he denounced asceticism. He made himself available to the masses, not only to heal (he was an accomplished herbalist, as well as a faith healer), but to inspire. He taught a form of meditation in prayer that even simple people could utilize. He founded no new movement. It has been shown that the classical Hasidic literature is mostly legend, and, in some cases, deliberate misrepresentation, reflecting political squabbles taking place half a century after his death. His closest students, however, did formulate a new approach to Kabbalah that became a movement. It is highly questionable that much of this is from Rabbi Israel himself. Some certainly is. Much is not.

What these students preached was not really new, but the application of these ideas was. The Ari had concentrated on the cosmic effects of the mitzvot and Torah life, the macrocosm. The students of Rabbi Israel turned that around. If we are affecting the macrocosm, and man is in God's image, we can and should affect the microcosm. Our Jewishness should make us happier; calm our fears, give a sense of belonging to something far greater and help us see significance everywhere, in everything. They emphasized the "magic" in our lives. God is everywhere; nothing is by accident; everything has meaning — not just for the universe, but for you and me.

They set up two tiers of followers. The first was an inner circle of spiritual leaders, who would go out and teach others how to feel the imminence of God and serve Him with joy. They had also a much larger outer circle; the common people, downtrodden and impoverished. They taught them that God desired our hearts more than our intellectual achievements. He could be served with a song, with a dance, or even by directing our everyday activities to thoughts of Him.

Kabbalistic ideas, already popular, were used to further each man and woman's spirituality. The idea of a future redemption was by no means abandoned, but the emphasis was now on an internal transformation. In the course of the next fifty years, the new movement, called Hasidism (from the Hebrew word meaning "pious") spread throughout Ukraine, White Russia, Poland, Hungary, and even into Lithuania, where it ran into great opposition from the scholarly community of the Lithuanian yeshivot. The scholars were uncomfortable about the new mass movement. Where would it lead? If the emphasis was on the emotional life, would it stay within the confines of Torah? Fears of a new Sabbateanism were expressed.

Those against the new movement were known as *mitnagdim* (opponents). The strife within the Jewish community was fierce until the mid-nineteenth century, but still exists to some extent even today. The students, and students of students of the Baal Shem Tov, founded different schools of Hasidism. Some emphasized joy, some contemplation, some love of fellow man, some public service, some ecstatic prayer, some emphasizing personal connection with charismatic spiritual leaders. The idea of dynasties of rebbes did not come in until after 1812, fifty-two years after the Baal Shem Tov, mostly due to Chabad propaganda and texts forgery.

Today, there are well over a thousand branches of Hasidism, some with only a few adherents, some with hundreds of thousands. In all, the inner life is the key, and joy is the tool to come to God —to finding ourselves. There was now a Kabbalah that lived where people lived. It might seem to be a superficial Kabbalah to some, but for others, it meant a constant deepening of the understanding, of the realization of God, of Life.

Sadly, in many Hasidic circles, customs, dress, and political alliances became more and more central. However, two remarkable figures, personal friends but different from each other, brought new vitality to the movement and founded unique approaches that still inspire large numbers of people to this day. That will be the next part of our story.

The eighteenth century saw Kabbalah largely put on a shelf, at best the province of the few. In some places, Kabbalah was still treasured but with the constant fear of another charlatan coming to pervert it. In fact, even though all traditional Jews pay lip service to the concept, many cringe at the idea of a Mashiach, fearing another Shabbatean ordeal. It has been seen that emotions get the better of us. Although the sages urge great restraint before recognizing anyone as Mashiach, that doesn't stop many people from saying, "It's different now. Everything is lined up. In fact, I can tell you who it is."

Anyone with a sense of history shudders at these words. All this has caused Kabbalah to be largely relegated to the realm of charlatans and the eccentric. A positive outcome of the Sabbatean debacle, however, was that Kabbalah had become, in most places, part of the common consciousness of the Jewish people. It permeated thoughts and even the folklore. Ideas like reincarnation were spoken about even by unlearned people. Concepts like the nature of the soul, fallen sparks, and the mitzvot were not seen as symbols or just laws, but as actively affecting a tikkun; a rectification of the universe became pervasive. The vocabulary of the East European Jew now included numerous Kabbalistic ideas, but they were not organized. It remained lore. It was as if a great tool was in their midst, but few knew how to use it. The "mainstream" rabbis were preaching either a soulless emphasis on the study of legal texts, or, worse, were expounding on the Aristotelian approach of RAMBAM's "guide," while having little real understanding themselves of that work. This was about to change. Change did come, although not all thought it was for the better. This is still a controversy in the Orthodox community. ◆◆◆

7 - Chabad-Lubavitch

It is a well-known phenomenon is history; some times and places produce great men, while other eras are fallow. Consider the late eighteenth century in America. Washington, Franklin, Adams, Jefferson, and a host of others established and forged the ideals of the United States. Since then, great statesmen have been rare. Similarly, the first three generations of Hasidic leaders produced an amazing array of, what Wiesel called, *Souls on Fire*. All were based on interpretations of the teachings of the Baal Shem Tov (or, more correctly, the teachings of his successor, the Mezricher Maggid), but each had taken these teachings in a different direction.

Unfortunately, the movement began to weaken after about fifty years. The first three generations had no dynasties. Still strong in numbers of adherents, dynasties of leaders began to emerge, with dynastic struggles. Sometimes the son or student who succeeded a leader was likewise a man of great stature. Sometimes, he was not. The leaders had begun, in many cases, to become figureheads. The follower (hasid) began to feel that his leader was doing the job for him. The hasid had no need for spiritual struggle; the "rebbe" did that on behalf of the community. (The title *rebbe* sprang up. A rabbi was primarily an expert in texts. A rebbe was supposed to be one who awakened the spirit. A rebbe may or may not have been an ordained rabbi, or, for that matter, even a scholar. Most, however, were.)

At this point, two unique figures appear. In this post, I will deal with the first. His name was Rabbi Shneur Zalman of Liadi (1745-1812). An accomplished scholar at age eighteen, who had already resolved a widespread dispute among the rabbis of White Russia on a point of Jewish law, he was perplexed by the growing tension between the great scholars of Lithuania and the spiritual giants who had founded and were leading the Hasidic movement. (From 1772, Lithuanian rabbis began excommunicating Hasidim, and even urging violence.) He visited the great learning center of Vilna and was greatly impressed. He visited the school of Rabbi Dov Ber of Mezritch, who had succeeded the Baal Shem Tov, and was "blown away" by the heights of spirituality of Rabbi Dov Ber and his disciples. He chose Mezritch. But, just as a nuclear reaction can make a bomb that destroys or can be used to generate electricity, he felt that emotion alone was too unstable. His incredible mind devised a process of contemplation, which, although primarily based on the Kabbalah of the Ari, was now converted into a spiritual-psychological science made accessible to all. He taught, and eventually recorded in a book (the *Tanya*), how the tension in the higher worlds is reflected within each person. One could then understand one's inner conflicts and (ideally) overcome evil, or at least keep evil at bay.

He described a system of contemplation designed to subdue one's physical lusts and urges. Emotions took a back seat to the mind governing the heart. Indeed, his successors debated whether emotions even had a place in divine service. Unlike other Hasidic rebbes, who often prayed with great ecstasy, Rabbi Shneur Zalman prayed frozen in place. The drama was going on inside of him.

He wrote extensively, reconciling the ideas of Kabbalah with those of philosophy (usually thought of as the opposite of Kabbalah), turning the process of deep thought into a spiritual awakening; the mind harnessing and controlling the tremendous power of the heart. He called his approach "Chabad," which is an acrostic of the names of the first three sefirot; Chochmah, Binah, and Daat — Wisdom, Understanding, and Knowledge. In his understanding, they meant, respectively, a seminal idea, expanding the idea with all its implications, and then connecting that idea with one's being. Spirituality, for him, meant not "flying to heaven," but fundamentally transforming one's being into a sanctuary for God.

The rebbe was not to be the problem solver in one's daily life, but a guide to help with one's struggles. He was to be "a shepherd who leads the sheep, not one who carries them." Each hasid was now left to set aside time for contemplation, to think about each mitzvah; not so much how it was meant to change the world, but how it was meant to change oneself. Rabbi Shneur Zalman had his detractors, even among other rebbes. Some felt that his approach was too cerebral. Some opposed his opening up of the deepest parts of Kabbalah for the average man or woman. Many resented his followers' assertion that Chabad was the real, essential form of Hasidism, with all other forms being watered down versions. But he inspired the masses of Jews of White Russia and beyond.

After his death in 1812, a great dispute arose. Some of his followers insisted there could be no successor, as he was such a unique figure. Others looked to one or another of his three sons as potential new rebbes. Still others looked to his closest disciple, Rabbi Aaaron of Strashely. By 1814, most had come to accept his son, Rabbi Dov Ber. This son moved to the village of Lubavitch.

Chabad-Lubavitch is now a worldwide movement (it is often quipped that wherever you go, you can find Lubavitch and Coca Cola). There have been seven Lubavitcher rebbes, each a unique figure. Since the third generation of Chabad, they have put the emphasis on outreach. Jews who are not affiliated are readily welcomed into Lubvavich. At the same time, there was a lessening of the emphasis on intellectual contemplation. The place of the rebbe also morphed into something more like other Hasidic rebbes, who were consulted on even the most mundane matters. Chabad Hasidim are also known, in recent decades, as being the most dedicated to the idea of Mashiach, although he is only rarely mentioned in the *Tanya* or other early Chabad texts. They see our actions and spiritual progress as bringing the entire universe to its Tikkun. This emphasis, however, along with the claims of many that their rebbe was, or even still is, Mashiach, has also brought them much opposition. As a result, many will have nothing to do with this movement. However, it cannot be denied that they do a lot for bringing Jews back to their roots. Chabad is what gave me my start in Judaism as well. Today, although all Chabad Hasidim study the *Tanya*, most have abandoned its system of contemplation in favor of outreach. Many also resent their promotion of Chabad ideology as "standard Judaism." Still, none of this tarnishes the image of the Great Rabbi Shneur Zalman.

A younger colleague (and friend) of Rabbi Shneur Zalman was about to launch a new and unique approach that has enthralled tens of thousands (including yours truly). It also "put the ball in the court" of the average man, but in ways not previously dreamed of. A different, unique, and controversial role for the rebbe also was a factor.

◆◆◆

8 - Rabbi Nachman of Breslov

In dealing with the late eighteenth century, we have seen that there were giants; great mystical leaders who brought the feeling of closeness to God to East European Jewry and beyond at a time when the Chassidic movement was in spiritual, if not numerical, decline. We have seen how Rabbi Shneur Zalman of Liadi strove to bring the job of devotion back to each individual, struggling to sanctify his or her life.

A younger colleague of Rabbi Shneir Zalman was Rabbi Nachman (1772-1810). His paternal grandfather had been a close disciple of the Baal Shem Tov. His mother, Feiga, was the Baal Shem Tov's granddaughter. Her brothers, two of the greatest tzaddikim of the time, called her the "Prophetess" because of her great spiritual accomplishments, clairvoyance, and her devotion to God. Hasidic leaders came to visit Nachman's parents while visiting Medzhibuzh, where the Baal Shem Tov had lived and was buried.

The young Nachman watched these great men and listened. As a child, he would try to emulate them, with nobody knowing. He tried acts of asceticism but found them to be of no avail. He later noted, "If you break a lust, you now are left with two lusts." He turned to individual prayer, *hitbodedut*, as the ultimate tool for self-mastery and connecting with God. He would go into the forests or take a rowboat out onto the river and spend entire days talking with God. He carefully hid all of his activities to be seen as ordinary. He had a profound sense of closeness with God. He would plead with God to draw him near. He later said that whatever could be accomplished with fasting and asceticism could be better accomplished with prayer. He developed a new take on mysticism.

Usually, we refer to the Bible and Talmud as the "revealed" Torah and Kabbalah as the "hidden" Torah. For him, however, there was a different definition. "Revealed" is what has been internalized; "hidden" is what one intuits but has not yet internalized. For a child just beginning school, the Five books of Moses are, as yet, "hidden." For an accomplished hasid, Zohar and Ari are "revealed."

There is yet a higher level, first to be intuited, and then internalized. There is a continuum. Likewise, prayer and study are a continuum. He taught his followers to make prayers out of what one has learned, Torah out of what one has experienced in prayer. This is to be done until your prayer has become "God's prayer," until your Torah has become "God's Torah." He made the shocking claim that the root of sin is not lust or the evil inclination, but rather depression. If one is depressed, one feels that one's actions, one's life, don't really matter, even to God. If one is happy, one feels close and significant. There is even a Biblical verse that reads, "Strength and Joy are in His place." But what kind of joy? Joy in doing mitzvot? That would be ideal. But most people can't, at first, achieve this. One must do even silly things (he would go outside, pick up a stick, and play-duel with little children). Once joy is achieved, it can be transferred to one's religious life.

He had a unique take on the Ari's concept of the "Empty Space." God has two ways of relating to our world. One is totally transcendent and unknowable. The other is to be "clothed" in the things and events of this world. Here is the "folly" of philosophy. The great questions are rooted in the dual nature of this relationship. Can God create a stone too heavy for Him to pick up? Nonsense! To be Omnipotent is to be *above* the empty space, while the terms "can" and "can't" only apply *below* the empty space. Man's response must be one of faith, and a sense of humor. The ultimate cannot be known, only sensed. Silent wonder should be our response to the great mysteries.

He raised many eyebrows with his approach to the commandments. He taught that they must be scrupulously adhered to but without the extreme stringency that characterized most Hasidic groups. "Keep the Shulchan Aruch (Code of Jewish Law), and no more. Flesh and blood can never observe the commandments fully. The only thing that can be perfect in our observance is our *desire* to serve God. Put the emphasis there!" On the other hand, he opposed the tendency of some to compromise on the requirements of Jewish Law in favor of ecstatic experiences. "You may turn my teachings every which way, but don't do violence to one sub-paragraph of the Shulchan Aruch." He taught renewal. Be a new being every day, even several times a day. Serve God in joy. You've sinned? Set aside a time in the day or a time in the week to deal with that. The rest of the time, be joyous. Over-regretting past deeds is a trap of "the other side" (evil).

Many Kabbalists, including the Ari, taught acts of "repair for one's sins, after repentance, to cleanse one's being." These generally consisted of numerous (often hundreds) fasts and acts of asceticism. Rabbi Nachman taught that after repentance, the ultimate repair is the joyous recitation of ten Psalms (16, 32, 41,42,57,77,90,105, 137, and 150). These are ten levels of melody, which can pierce depression and evil and bring holiness to the surface. How did these ideas become a movement? Why were he and his followers persecuted? That will be our next installment.

◆◆◆

9 - Difficulties and Transformation

Another pivotal teaching of Rabbi Nachman was that anything important will come with obstacles (*meni'ot*). The letters of *meni'ot* can be rearranged to spell *ne'imot* (pleasant). In order to merit arriving at holiness, God gives us obstacles to overcome, making us worthy to "enter the gates" of holiness. Moreover, God Himself is hidden in the obstacle. If something comes too easily, it's probably not worth it, or even bad. Moreover, leaders who speak great truths will have opposition. Those who oppose Rabbi Nachman will see him as a terrible person who *must* be opposed. But God uses this situation to push away the insincere, allowing only those who truly seek Truth to approach.

This is similar to what I wrote in my article about converts, that they are initially informed that persecution is the norm for our people. If they say, "I wish I may be worthy of partaking in this persecution," they are accepted immediately. For Rabbi Nachman, literal converts, Jews who had strayed from the path of observance but were now returning and becoming observant, as well as non-spiritual Jews, were essentially in the same boat. They both needed to find someone who could open their eyes to God.

The Land of Israel was very central to his thinking. Many of the early Hasidic leaders de-emphasized it, reinterpreting it as a metaphor for spirituality. Rabbi Nachman disagreed and saw the Holy Land as the quintessence of spirituality "in place," just as Shabbat was the quintessence of spirituality "in time."

Suddenly, in 1798, Rabbi Nachman picked himself up and began an amazing journey to the Land Israel. He only had enough money to get as far as Odessa. With few provisions, accompanied by one of his followers, he set out on the perilous journey. It was the middle of the Napoleonic Wars. He even hinted that there was a spiritual connection between himself and Napoleon. The seas were fraught with danger. There are entire books written about his journey. He, at one point, found himself prisoner on a Turkish warship. They wanted to sell him as a slave. He was ransomed by a wealthy Jew in Rhodes. There was misadventure after misadventure, but these were *meni'ot*. He had to break them in order to break through the forces which kept us in exile, spiritually as well as physically.

The journey, round trip, took a little over a year. On the eve of Rosh Hashanah, he arrived in Haifa. He walked a few paces and made a startling statement. "I have received a perception of God that none have ever perceived. I have been given a gift of Rosh Hashanah. From now on, all my followers must come to me for Rosh Hashanah." The meaning of this is far beyond my understanding. However, one can understand it to a degree. Rosh Hashanah is the death of the old year, the death of the old me, and the birth of a new year and a new me. But it's not simply about changing. It's about transformation to ultimate good. Like the moon seeming about to disappear then suddenly reappearing and achieving great brightness, so man has his cycles.

The tzaddik can be instrumental in guiding that transformation, while he is in battle not only with Evil, but with God's own attribute of stern judgement. The tzaddik endeavors to change judgement to mercy, dread to joy. In the presence of the tzaddik, Rosh Hashanah is a joyous cosmic celebration of rebirth, rather than the traditional concept of a Day of Awe and judgment. When he returned to

Ukraine, followers began to flock to him for Rosh Hashanah. Even since his passing, many still flock to his resting place for these days.

In Judaism, many are opposed, but many are for, the concept of visiting the graves of the righteous. I hope to write a separate post explaining the various views on this topic. One thing must be clear: we *never* pray *to* the tzaddik.

In recent years, some eighty thousand people come yearly to the city of Uman in Ukraine. Of the seventeen times I personally have been there, thirteen have been on Rosh Hashanah. These were unforgettable, transformational experiences. Even in times of political turmoil, followers of Rabbi Nachman make the pilgrimage, coming from the US, Israel, UK, Canada, France — everywhere. There are many people who oppose this on various grounds. One Jewish newspaper published a scathing hate-filled critique of the "Cult of Uman." But for Rabbi Nachman's followers, this is just another obstacle; more darkness to be overcome, penetrated, and broken.

Many famous rabbis make the trip. None are sorry. Services are conducted there not only in the Hasidic, Ashkenazi rite, but Sephardic and Yemenite as well. Breslov is today a truly multi-cultural movement. As Rabbi Nachman hid his customs, these are not a major part of Breslov tradition, and each adherent keeps his own ways. One year, when I was unable to attend, I spoke to my teacher, Rabbi ND Kiwak. He said, "One must do everything possible to go and take part. But, if it's ten minutes before sundown on Rosh Hashanah, and you're still not there, connect yourself from wherever you are."

For Breslovers, Rosh Hashanah is seen as a most joyous day of coming to God, of transforming our lives. Rabbi Nachman once said about crying on Rosh Hashanah, "Yes, tears of joy."

In the next two years after returning from the Land of Israel, two people came into his life who were central to the development of the movement. One was a bitter opponent; one a faithful friend and disciple. That will be my next post.

◆◆◆

10 - Attempting Peace

When Rabbi Nachman returned from the Holy Land, before returning home, he visited many of the senior Hasidic leaders in Ukraine and as far as White Russia, where he attempted to make peace between Rabbi Shneur Zalman of Liadi and his bitter rival, Rabbi Avraham of Kalisk, head of the Hasisdic community in Tiberias. He was warmly received by all, especially Rabbi Aryeh Leib of Shpola, who was universally loved and known as the Shpoler Zeida (grandfather). He showed the young Rabbi Nachman unbounded affection.

Rabbi Nachman returned to the town he lived in but soon and unexpectedly moved with his family to Zlatopola, a town next to Shpola. Rabbi Nachman was not pleased with the local cantor, saying he was praying not for God but to impress his wife. The cantor was furious. He was a follower of the Shpoler. He went to his rebbe and complained. The attitude of the Shpoler took a strong turn against Rabbi Nachman. The last decade of Rabbi Nachman's life was plagued with constant denunciation from his erstwhile friend. What caused the Shpoler to behave this way? Was it personal? Ideological? There is no way of knowing. But Rabbi Nachman saw it as a great barrier around him, which anyone seeking the light of his teachings would need to break through. "I knew *someone* would be used this way, but I'm surprised that it's he," said Rabbi Nachman.

He spent two years in Zlatipola, under constant persecution. He then moved to Breslov (Bratzlav), which, at that time, was a thriving mercantile center (it was later largely destroyed by the great fire of 1810 and has been a backwater since). This scenario has repeated time and time again. Seemingly devout people will suddenly go on the offensive against Rabbi Nachman. There have even been cases of bloodshed. From the perspective of Breslovers, these people are, sadly, allowing themselves to be used by dark powers.

Now let us turn our attention elsewhere. Rabbi Natan of Nemerov (a town near Breslov) was the son of a wealthy family. He had a great mind and was chosen by Rabbi David Tzvi Aurbach, the regional rabbi, to be his son-in-law, with the thought of having Rabbi Natan succeed him. Rabbi Natan's parents were opposed to the Hasidic movement, as was his father-in-law, but the young Natan felt something was missing. He loved to study Torah, but nevertheless felt that he was not close to God. He had Hasidic friends who urged him in the Hasidic direction. He visited many Hasidic leaders. He was impressed by them but felt their followers "didn't get it."

He eventually came to the holy Rabbi Levi Yitzchak of Berdichev. The two men became close, but the young Natan felt that despite the rabbi's greatness and vast insights, his students were spiritually shallow. One Saturday night, the followers decided, in the Hasidic manner, to have a small gathering where they would eat, sing, and discuss their rabbi's teachings. They cast lots to see who would buy the bagels for the event, and it fell on Natan. The young rabbi, who had just turned twenty-two, was on his way to the bakery, thinking, "Is this the meaning of life? Bagels?" He walked into the synagogue and began saying Psalms. He fell asleep. As he slept, he dreamed of a ladder going to Heaven. He began climbing but fell. This happened several times. Each time he got a little further but would fall again. A window opened in Heaven. He saw a young man with a red beard, who said to him "Keep climbing, but just hold on tight." He awoke, immediately left Berdichev, and went home to Nemerov. He was dejected, broken.

When he got home, he saw at the synagogue an old friend who was, uncharacteristically, praying with great joy and fervor. Rabbi Natan asked what happened. The friend told him that a young Hasidic rebbe had just moved into the nearby town of Breslov. He had visited him and become inspired. Rabbi Natan traveled there and immediately recognized Rabbi Nachman as the man he had seen in his dream. Rabbi Nachman said to him, "We know each other from long ago, but we haven't seen each other in a very a long time." This was not new. It was Moses and Joshua; it was the Ari and Rabbi Hayyim Vital; it was the greater light (the Sun) and the lesser light (the Moon).

Over the next eight years, Rabbi Natan was Rabbi Nachman's constant companion, writing down every word he said. Nearly everything we have from Rabbi Nachman comes only through Rabbi Natan. "Honor him," said Rabbi Nachman, "for, if not for him, nothing of me would remain."

Rabbi Natan was disowned by his family. His wife reluctantly stayed with him, but the relationship soured. Not only had he become Hasidic, but he had also joined a rebbe who was being persecuted by a much-loved figure. Rabbi Natan became poor financially. He quipped, "When I had to go over to eating with a wooden spoon, it took a long time until I could taste the food again." But he was now rich spiritually. He was absorbing and reflecting the light of the tzaddik. He was, essentially, an extension of the tzaddik. He went to a mountaintop outside of Breslov and prayed with great wailing, "Master of the universe, a fire burns in Breslov! Please make it burn in my heart!"

Rabbi Natan was to publish two full-length volumes of Rabbi Nachman's teachings, and other additional smaller books including one with the rabbi's off the cuff remarks, a biography of Rabbi Nachman, and a collection of Rabbi Nachman's amazing Ancient Tales, which was really allegorical Kabbalistic stories. Rabbi Natan also wrote and published a book of his own private prayers, and an extensive commentary on the Code of Jewish Law that applied Rabbi Nachman's insights to every aspect of Jewish tradition, as well as to life in general. (The edition I have is in fifteen volumes.) But Rabbi Nachman made it clear that his work was not only for his followers, and not only for his contemporaries. He had much bigger plans. That will be my next story.

◆◆◆

11 - Rabbi Nachman's Final Days

At this point, we need to digress a bit. There are many areas of Jewish Law and Tradition that are subject to different interpretations. One relates to the issue of visiting the graves of holy people. Many Jewish philosophers opposed this strongly. RAMBAM opposed *ever* visiting a grave, but there are numerous references in Talmud to the practice. As a result, many permit, or even encourage, such visits, but without prayers being said to anyone but God.

Another issue is, are the dead involved with the needs of the living? Many say no. But there are numerous Talmudic statements to the contrary. Rachel was buried on the roadside "so she may pray for her children when they go into exile." In fact, "Rachel crying for her children" is mentioned in the Bible. Jeremiah is said to have prayed at the graves of the patriarchs for them to intercede on behalf of the people. How about the living helping the dead? Here, too, many rejected this in the strongest terms. But others saw this as basic; we may do acts of charity and prayer that will aid the departed.

There are two Talmudic stories that put this into sharp focus. When King David's rebellious son, Absalom, is killed in battle, David cries, "Absalom, Absalom, my son..." He says eight times either "Absalom" or "my son." The Talmud says that in doing so, he lifted Absalom from the seven levels of Gehinnom (purgatory) and brought him to Paradise.

Another story concerns Elisha ben Avuyah, a Talmudic sage who turned away from God. There are numerous stories as to why and how this occurred. His student, Rabbi Meir, still remained close with him, however. "He [Rabbi Meir] found a pomegranate, ate the fruit, and discarded the rind." When Elisha ben Avuyah died, Rabbi Meir was given a difficult choice from Heaven: "Shall he go into non-existence, or descend to Gehinnom, and eventually attain Paradise?" Rabbi Meir chose the latter, and smoke rose from Elisha's grave. Another rabbi, Rabbi Yochanan, said to Rabbi Meir, "This is your honor for your teacher? When I die, I'll take him out of Gehinnom, and bring him into Paradise."

The day Rabbi Yochanan died, the smoke ceased from Elisha's grave. This idea is greatly expanded in the Kabbalistic literature. The Zohar states that in our daily prayers, where we suddenly go from a standing posture to prostrating (either literally or at least sitting with our face on our arm), the tzaddikim go from the highest heaven (achieved during the Amidah prayer) and jump into Gehinnom to rescue those who are trapped there. As astounding as this idea is, Rabbi Nachman was about to take it much further.

In 1768, there was a huge massacre of Jews in the city of Uman, perpetrated by Cossacks, who gave the Jews the option of conversion or death. All died except for a handful who hid in a cave. After three days of horror, those who hid came out to discover a huge number of dead: thirty thousand or more. They dug a mass grave, burying the martyrs. Rabbi Nachman, on one of his journeys, passed through Uman. He stopped at the mass grave, stood in a particular spot for a long time, and turned to his student who was with him, saying, "Here it would be good to lie."

At this point, Rabbi Nachman began to divide his time among giving life to the living, inspiring his followers with hope and joy, and bringing the dead to God. He announced that his intent was to "fix" *all* souls. He further swore a solemn oath, that, after his death, anyone who came to his grave would give a coin to charity and recite the ten psalms he had previously taught as a remedy for the soul. "I will go to the length and breadth of the universe to help that person. By his ear locks, I will take him out from the lowest hell and lower." This was understood to mean both the "hellish" side of life, as well as the hereafter.

He spent the last six months of his life in Uman. He was buried at the very spot where he had stood in prayer and meditation. The great spiritual arousal that one experiences there cannot be described. Those "rabbis" who oppose the pilgrimage, are telling us more about themselves than about Rabbi Nachman. His teachings are an amazing combination of how to live a joyous life as well as the eternal meaning of life beyond our limited life span. The world we see is an illusion, the only reality is God. Rabbi Nachman showed how to remove the hand from over our eyes and see the reality that we never normally see. How to find happiness, fulfillment, meaning, every moment of every day — how was this to be done? What does it mean for you and me?

◆◆◆

12 - His Legacy

In the eight years that Rabbi Natan spent with Rabbi Nachman, he not only went through a spiritual transformation on a personal level but enabled future generations to see and appreciate his experiences. Rabbi Nachman would take him along on trips to distant places, as well as wander the hills around the city of Breslov, revealing his visions, his hopes for each individual, and the world. Rabbi Nachman revealed many awesome teachings, some public, some private, and some that were to be kept secret among his followers. On the one hand, Rabbi Nachman seemed pessimistic, but it was, ironically, a pessimism with a huge degree of optimism. "Heresy and atheism are coming into the world. A time is coming when a simple Jew who washes his hands before eating bread (a requirement of Jewish law) will be as unique as the Baal Shem Tov in his time."

His students were astounded. "Maybe we shouldn't have children?"

He answered, "No, you do your part. When the Messiah comes, everyone and everything will be rectified."

He saw the War of Gog and Magog not as a military struggle, but a spiritual, ideological struggle to maintain faith and hope in the face of hostility, secularism, and negativity. What of the all-pervasive antisemitism that Jews faced? The Messiah would be able to do nothing until reconciliation took place between the Jews and the Nations (this was a very radical idea). The world, in fact, was always approaching perfection. One had to know how to read between the lines of events.

At age thirty-five, Rabbi Nachman contracted tuberculosis. He was told he had a few months to live but lived more than three years. During this time, he remained joyful, assuring his followers that he was not leaving them but only entering a "different room." On the contrary, he would be able to do more when free of the physical body. ("It's time to take this shirt off.")

During this time, he began to tell stories, but not ordinary stories. They sound like fairy tales, replete with kings, queens, princesses, and pirates. There are thirteen main stories, plus a host of more minor ones. They are allegories of life on the personal and cosmic levels. They speak of birth, death, and restoration. Most begin with an ideal situation destroyed by some cataclysm that finally works out to a greater perfection than had been previously known. Buber called them a "literary genre all their own." Others compare them to the writings of Kafka, who was deeply influenced by Rabbi Nachman. Although Rabbi Nachman gave hints as to their meanings, he stressed that "entire worlds" were hidden in each word. He quipped, "People say that stories put you to sleep. Mine wake you up. People say, you can't become pregnant from a story. From mine, you do." He instructed Rabbi Natan to publish the stories together with a translation into the Yiddish vernacular, so that a barren woman would be able to read them and become pregnant. (I actually saw this in my own family, but that is a story for another day.)

In Rabbi Nachman's time, visiting with a tzaddik had become a ritual. One would enter his study, hand him a note with one's requests, and receive a blessing and perhaps advice. So it remains in most Hasidic groups. Not Rabbi Nachman. One would enter his study. He would say, "*Heint, zog.*" (Now, start talking). The person would tell their life story, from his earliest memories, including all their successes and failures. Many derided this, calling his followers *viduinikers* (confessors). But people visited Rabbi Nachman and shared their hearts saw their life story changing before their eyes. People would come in bowing with sorrow, but go out standing upright, ready to begin anew.

As I have noted, he wanted to be buried in Uman, near the martyrs of 1768. In early 1810, a fire broke out in Breslov it never recovered from. He was forced to leave his home in the middle of the night. The following day, a messenger came from Uman with a letter from the heads of the town offering him a home among them. He turned pale. "Shoyn!" (Already!) He was being called to his death. He lived in Uman another six months. There were several major heretics in Uman who had made a pact never to mention God. Rabbi Nachman mysteriously befriended them and spent many hours playing chess with them. This added to the mystery and to the opposition, but he didn't care.

One of his students asked, "Rabbi, what do you have to do with *them*?"

He answered, "And what do I have to do with you?" His message was for all; devout or not, Jewish or not. "Everyone needs me, even the other Hasidic leaders. Everyone needs me, even the gentiles."

At his last Rosh HaShanah, two weeks before his death at age thirty-eight (just like the Ari), he gave a long, two-hour teaching about remaining happy and hopeful, engaging always in heartfelt prayer and staying close with friends. Rabbi Nachman would remain among us. He died on the fourth day of the Sukkot festival and was buried the next day at the spot he had chosen years before. Miraculous events were reported from his funeral. His burial place has been a site for pilgrimage ever since, but what now? How could his followers, especially Rabbi Natan, who was connected with his teacher's heart and soul, go on? What does anyone do who has lost the focus of their life? That will be the next part of the story.

◆◆◆

13 - Rabbi Natan Carries the Movement

When Rabbi Nachman passed away in 1810, Rabbi Natan was only thirty years old. Many of the other followers were much older. Some had even been Hasdic leaders in their own rights before coming to Rabbi Nachman. No one knew quite what to do. Dynasties had not yet become a feature of Hasidism. In most groups, when a rebbe died, his followers would scatter, and each would seek a new rebbe. A few did just that, but most realized that Rabbi Nachman's teachings were so unique, anyone else would be disappointing at best.

The consensus was that they had enough recorded teachings of Rabbi Nachman to live out their lives in a satisfactory way. But Rabbi Natan remembered that Rabbi Nachman had said, "My fire will glow until the Mashiach." He set out not only to preserve Rabbi Nachman's legacy, but to spread it. He published another volume of the rebbe's teachings that had been revealed after the first volume of Likkutei Moharan had been printed several years earlier. He printed original prayers based on the rebbe's teachings. He traveled around the countryside, urging the rebbe's followers to meet regularly in Uman. They would visit Rabbi Nachman's resting place, study and pray together, and give and receive encouragement.

Lo and behold, the movement began to grow. Young people were moved and inspired by the teachings. But opposition wasn't far off. Rabbi Nachman had been hounded by the Shpoler Zeida; but it was personal, nonviolent opposition to his unusual ways. Rabbi

Nachman's followers had been derisively dubbed *viddduiniks* (confessors) because they would tell him their secret thoughts and deeds. Now, a new pejorative name was born, *Toiter Hasidim* (Dead Hasidim), as they followed the teachings of a person no longer physically alive.

Rabbi Natan was urged by many Ukrainian Hasidic leaders to accept the title of rebbe, and all would be well. Rabbi Natan steadfastly refused. "I *know* I'm not the rebbe." Although the conventional wisdom is that he was faulted for not becoming a rebbe, recent research has shown that the opposite was the case. Breslov was, in fact, the first Hasidic group to remain intact after the rebbe's demise. This scared many. (Within a decade, this became the norm in most groups). Terrible rumors began to circulate.

Rabbi Natan was often red faced with excitement and enthusiasm. People began to say that he was a drunkard. A story circulated that he often addressed his followers with a female on his lap. It was actually his infant granddaughter. In 1834, he opened a synagogue for his group, now known as Breslover Hasidim. For some, this was too much. Rabbi Nachman had taught that Truth will always be persecuted. This was fulfilled in Rabbi Natan. A prominent Hasidic rabbi, Moshe of Savran, declared Breslov to be heresy and that Rabbi Natan should be killed. Attempts were made on his life. The Savraner's cause was supported by... was supported by many other Ukrainian Hasidic rabbis and rebbes. Rabbi Natan's opponents appealed to the authorities that he was planning to destroy society and rebel against the czar. He was tried for treason. His opponents hoped he would be sent to Siberia. The heretics Rabbi Nachman had befriended years earlier had government connections. They intervened on Rav Natan's behalf. His sentence was commuted to exile to his boyhood town of Nemirov, but all who came were in danger. Stones were thrown at them, and threats were made against their families. Some were actually killed. All but five had to break their connection with Rabbi Natan, at least temporarily.

This continued for some five years, until the rabbi of Savran died. Rabbi Natan continued his prayers, his printing, and his teaching. One of his students remarked, "When disaster was looming, we saw no difference in Rabbi Natan's face between the time it started until it ended. We only saw a difference from the time it started until he had prayed about it. Once he prayed, he felt that all had been taken care of."

Rabbi Natan wrote extensively, not about his trials and tribulations, but about joy in serving God. He wrote how to find God in all things at all times. One of the heretics asked him if he would like to arrange for his opponents to be arrested and punished (they had sufficient political clout for that). Rabbi Natan refused, quoting the Talmud: "It is better to be among the persecuted than among the persecutors." The persecution eased greatly in 1837/38 after the passing of the Savraner, but Ukrainian Hasidim remained suspicious of the new movement until fairly recently. Between 1838 and his own death in 1844, Rabbi Natan resumed his travels and encouragement. He visited other lands, where he was warmly welcomed, especially in Poland.

There remained opposition beneath the surface in Ukraine, albeit at a lower level. His neighbor across the street, who was a follower of Rabbi Natan's opponent, was asked why he didn't join in the persecution. He said, "I wanted to, but every night I hear him arise at midnight and recite prayers bemoaning the destruction of the Temple and praying for its restoration. I'm pulled from my bed by his voice, and I also begin to pray. How can I then throw rocks at him in the morning?"

He died late Friday afternoon on December 20, 1844. His final address to his students in Breslov urged them to stay together and print and reprint the books of Rabbi Nachman's teachings, as "even one page can be a life raft for future generations." He was buried Saturday night. His erstwhile enemies came to the funeral, not quite sure why they had ever opposed him. Word of his passing reached Uman on Sunday. The messengers were told that they already knew. How? Rabbi Natan had a longtime friend in Uman named Rabbi Naftali. He had a dream Friday night in which he saw Rabbi Natan running. "Natan, where are you running?" asked Rabbi Naftali. "Me? Straight to the rebbe."

For the next sixty years, Breslov remained an obscure local sect, but that was about to change, because a young man found a book. That is the next part of the story.

When we are faced with problems, when we are attacked and persecuted for no reason, should we break? Should we give up? Rabbi Natan said to hold on tight to one's faith in God and maintain a forgiving tolerance. Joy will overcome sadness; truth will overcome falsehood. Just pray and see your problems as having been solved.

◆◆◆

14 - The Light Expands

Rabbi Natan passed away in 1844. Small groups of Breslovers continued in obscure Ukrainian towns. Opposition existed, but at least it was non-violent. There was little hope of becoming a mass-movement in that environment. The tremendous sense of spirituality, the study of Torah and ecstatic prayer that had been taught by Rabbi Nachman, seemed doomed to oblivion. The increasing secularism in Russia and Ukraine, along with the widespread pogroms perpetrated against the Jews in the first years of the twentieth century, caused many Jews to flee Ukraine, where they had lived for some eight hundred years. Mass immigration to America occurred at this time (this is the time when my grandparents came to the US). However, a significant number went to the Holy Land, then a Turkish province. As Rabbi Nachman had greatly praised the Holy Land and had made a pilgrimage there, and a similar pilgrimage was made by Rabbi Natan many years later, several pivotal Breslov leaders moved to Jerusalem.

One was asked, "How can you leave Rabbi Nachman's burial place?" He responded, "I doubt if your grandchildren will even have heard of Rabbi Nachman or his burial place." Those were prophetic words. As I wrote in the last article, Rabbi Natan said, "I believe that one page of Rabbi Nachman's words can be a life raft." The Breslovers, though a tiny, persecuted group, continued to print and distribute the literary treasures that continued to give them joy and a sense of closeness with

God and Torah, despite the icy reception these words found among their brethren.

I was once told by a young man who was distributing Breslov books, "I believe that every book has an address." One such book found its addressee in the unlikely location of Lublin, Poland. Rabbi Yitzchak Breiter (1886-1943) was a student at a yeshiva in Lublin. He had never heard of Breslov or Rabbi Nachman. One day, he "happened" to pick up a book someone had left on his desk. It was the writings of Rabbi Nachman. He looked and was overcome by a feeling of wonder and enthusiasm. He studied the book diligently that day, but the next day it was gone; it had simply vanished. Sometime later, he found another book, a commentary on the first. He devoured it. The title page said it was put out in Breslov. Breslov? Where was that? He wrote letters to Breslau in Germany that remained unanswered. He saw the city of Uman mentioned. He assumed that this was a place in ancient Israel. He began telling his friends about the wonderful thoughts he had discovered in these books. He spoke longingly of Uman, which he assumed to be in the Holy Land. A fellow student passed by and overheard what he was saying. "Holy Land? It's in Ukraine, just a few hundred miles from here. I'm from that area. There are a bunch of crazies there that study these books and follow a dead rebbe."

Rabbi Yitzchak was excited. He now had an "address." He wrote a letter to a Jewish bookstore in Uman asking for more information. Alas, the owner of the store was an opponent of the Breslovers. The letter remained untouched for many weeks. One day, one of the Breslover leaders in Uman came into the shop, and the proprietor handed him the letter. "Has someone not from this region discovered our treasures?" He shared this with his friends and colleagues. They all undertook writing the young scholar words of encouragement, words of insight.

Rabbi Yitzchak was amazed to receive a large bundle of letters filled with light and life. He began preaching these ideas all over Poland and gathered several thousand followers. This was unprecedented in the history of the movement. Persecution of the movement was unheard of in the Polish Jewish community. When the great Rabbi Meir Shapiro of Lublin opened his magnificent yeshivah in 1924, he welcomed Rabbi Yitzchak to use it as a central gathering place for the movement. On Rosh Hashanah, when Ukrainian Breslovers gathered in Uman, thousands of Polish Breslovers gathered in Lublin, and Rabbi Shapiro not only prayed with them, but led the Musaf services… year after year!

Eli Wiesel writes that his first encounter with the teachings of Rabbi Nachman was in a concentration camp, where the Breslover inmates would encourage the others to have faith and find joy in life, even in those horrendous circumstances. Although Rabbi Yitzchak Breiter perished in Treblinka after having been a source of inspiration in the Warsaw ghetto, his surviving students spread Breslov all over the world. It was one of his works that I found in Cincinnati in 1975 that inspired me to study these teachings and which reshaped my life. Indeed, it was for me a life raft. Every book has an address.

◆◆◆

15 - Controversy Often Challenges Greatness

Some of you have been asking why Rabbi Nachman and his teachings were, and to a degree, still are, persecuted. In thinking about it, I realized that this question is, indeed, pertinent to the entire theme of this group. Community can be a great benefit, or it can be a straitjacket of conformity, stifling everything, especially spiritual growth.

There are several reasons for the opposition to Rabbi Nachman. I will take them one by one. Some of you may have come across the name of Rabbi Nasan Maimon. When he was a young man, he worked as a computer systems analyst. He had with him at work a volume of the teachings of Rabbi Nachman. His boss, who was also Hasidic, from a group not opposed to Breslov, picked the book up and read on the title page great praise for Rabbi Nachman. He immediately threw the book down on the desk. Rabbi Maimon asked for an explanation. "Nobody is that great. Nobody is as great as *my* rebbe, and he's not so much."

While it is true that the Talmud speaks of a *yeridat hadorot* (a spiritual decline in all generations after Sinai), this cannot be taken as rigid rule. Great luminaries have appeared throughout history. Most people would agree with this... but not about now. My wife and I became attracted to Judaism through different teachers. Yet, both of us have been told, "You can't imagine the awesome level of the average Jew one hundred years ago." Someone with any rudimentary knowledge of Jewish history would understand how totally nonsensical that statement is.

Similarly, I was once in the home of a pious man, whose grandfather was a very prominent Hungarian rabbi. He showed me his grandparents' wedding pictures. I was surprised that there was no *mechitzah* (partition) between the men and the women. He looked at me and said, "You're comparing our women to the women of two generations ago?" (That was to say, they were all very pious and modest then; not like "our" brazen women). In my opinion, this attitude not only prevents progress, but also keeps us from marveling at the great spiritual giants among us. Rabbi Nachman *can't* be seen as the remarkable person he was, because he lived only two hundred years ago. If five hundred, he'd have a chance. It was, at one time, common for great tzaddikim to sing their own praise. This was not done out of arrogance, but in order to let the people know to whom to turn for help. In Rabbi Nachman's time, this was no longer common, but Rabbi Nachman did praise himself and his work. At the same time, those close to him spoke of his great humility. Outsiders, however, saw him as a braggart. It's like Einstein being rejected by science because he dared to disagree with Newton, who lived over two hundred and fifty years earlier.

Another, more spiritual factor lies in Rabbi Nachman's teaching that the more righteous the person, the more he becomes like polished mirror. Others then see their reflection in him and don't like what they see. They ascribe the failing to the tzaddik when they are actually seeing themselves. Hasidism's heyday was in the past, and Hasidim were now content with mediocrity. Rabbi Nachman tried to give it back its soul. Many saw this as impossible. It threatened the stature of recognized rebbes. He upset the apple cart. In my opinion, it needed upsetting. ◆◆◆

16 - Kabbalah Today

What is the state of Kabbalah today? Hasidim are centered on the ideas of Kabbalah, but, for the most part, not on studying the primary texts. Only people on an advanced level would touch the actual Zohar or writings of the Ari. The big exception is Breslov where Kabbalah is freely studied. Chabad is very Kabbalah-centered, but only as seen through the lens of Chabad Hasidism. Only the most advanced study Zohar or the actual writings of the Ari.

There is a video of Rabbi Ashlag, who wrote a Hebrew translation of the Zohar and a commentary urging the Lubavitcher rebbe to encourage his followers to study Zohar daily. His entreaty was met with refusal. Yet, Kabbalistic ideas abound in Chabad literature and thought. In Middle Eastern Sepharadic circles, even the uneducated will read the Zohar, without knowing its meaning. They find the recitation alone to be inspiring. Rabbis in those communities are generally well versed in Zohar, and Kabbalistic rituals are common in those circles. Sadly, however, many present-day Sepharadic rabbis have studied in Ashkenazic Yeshivot, and little that is Sepharadic remains with them other than their pronunciation of Hebrew. Among non-Hasidic Ashkenazim, Kabbalah is either put on a shelf or actively opposed. At best, a sterilized, non-emotional Kabbalah is studied.

In Modern Orthodox circles, Kabbalah is usually rejected outright. This is not true in Israel, as the writings of Rav Kook are almost totally based on Kabbalah. "New-agers" rediscovered Kabbalah, but mostly as a way of "spacing out," often in combination with drugs and promiscuity. The mid twentieth century saw the birth of various Kabbalah centers, teaching a “new-age” Kabbalah. For example, the Messianic Era becomes the "Age of Aquarius.” Observance of the mitzvot is absent, and Kabbalah becomes a quasi-philosophical/self-help, universalist movement.

On the positive side, the Open Orthodox movement sees Kabbalah as a major part of Torah and Jewish life, recognizing that it is, in fact, the soul of Judaism. Non-Orthodox movements have historically rejected Kabbalah, but that is now changing. An ethical understanding of Judaism, as preached by classical Reform, or an historical approach, championed by conservatives, solves few people's spiritual longings and questioning. Several people have come forward in both those movements with messages that spiritual truths are to be found in Kabbalah. The urge to find God is strong. Ironically, it is often the local Orthodox rabbis who try to squelch this impulse. I know many people who were attracted to Judaism because of the Kabbalistic writings, especially those of Rabbi Nachman, only to be told by their rabbis that it is forbidden to read these works. Indeed, the ArtScroll editions of classical Torah commentaries have Kabbalah carefully censored out. I don't believe that this can continue. Numerous people seek God through His Torah. Besides the roadblocks put in the way of those seeking conversion, the next hurdle is a Judaism that is essentially "Do this, and don't do that," with incredibly shallow explanations of why that is good. Eventually, people will simply not stand for it. I am told that in many parts of the US, spiritually sterile Modern Orthodoxy is already being replaced with Chabad. I see this as a step in the right direction. Like when Hasidism first began and was persecuted by the yeshiva heads of Central and Eastern Europe; the people "voted with their feet," and non-Hasidic Orthodoxy was mostly left in the dust in many areas. In the words of Rabbi Nachman in one of his stories, "Keep your treasures! Make use of them!"

◆◆◆

◆◆◆

May the All Merciful One restore His Crown to its former glory. May we rejoice in His Commandments and see the fulfillment of the verse *"And many nations shall go, and they shall say, "Come, let us go up to the Lord's mount, to the house of the G-d of Jacob, and let Him teach us of His ways, and we will go in His paths, for out of Zion shall the Torah come forth, and the word of the Lord from Jerusalem."* (Isaiah 2:3) Amen.

◆◆◆

ABOUT THE AUTHOR

◆◆◆

Rabbi Yaakov HaLevi s"t, is in fact a pen name. The author has decided to release his book under an assumed name since the information in this book is controversial, and loaded with hot-button topics. As described in the book, most rabbis would not only shy away from these issues but would also shun anyone who raises them. Rabbi Yaakov HaLevi is a brilliant Torah scholar with a wide array of knowledge in many areas including Torah, Talmud, halacha, world history, and Jewish History. The Rabbi has studied and corresponded with some of the greatest Torah minds of both this generation and the previous one. His source-based approach, wide knowledge base, and unique life experience lend a perspective like none-other in this day and age.

Made in the USA
Middletown, DE
05 September 2023